MANDALA ADULT COLOURING BOOK FOR STRESS RELIEF

BY ACE COLORING

IN PARTNERSHIP WITH SILVERBAY PUBLISHING

CUT OUT BLEED PAGE

SHARE YOUR COLORING ON INSTAGRAM:

@ACECOLORING

OR BY USINGS THE HASHTAG

ACECOLORING

CONTACT US VIA EMAIL:
JOE@SILVERBAYPUBLISHING.COM

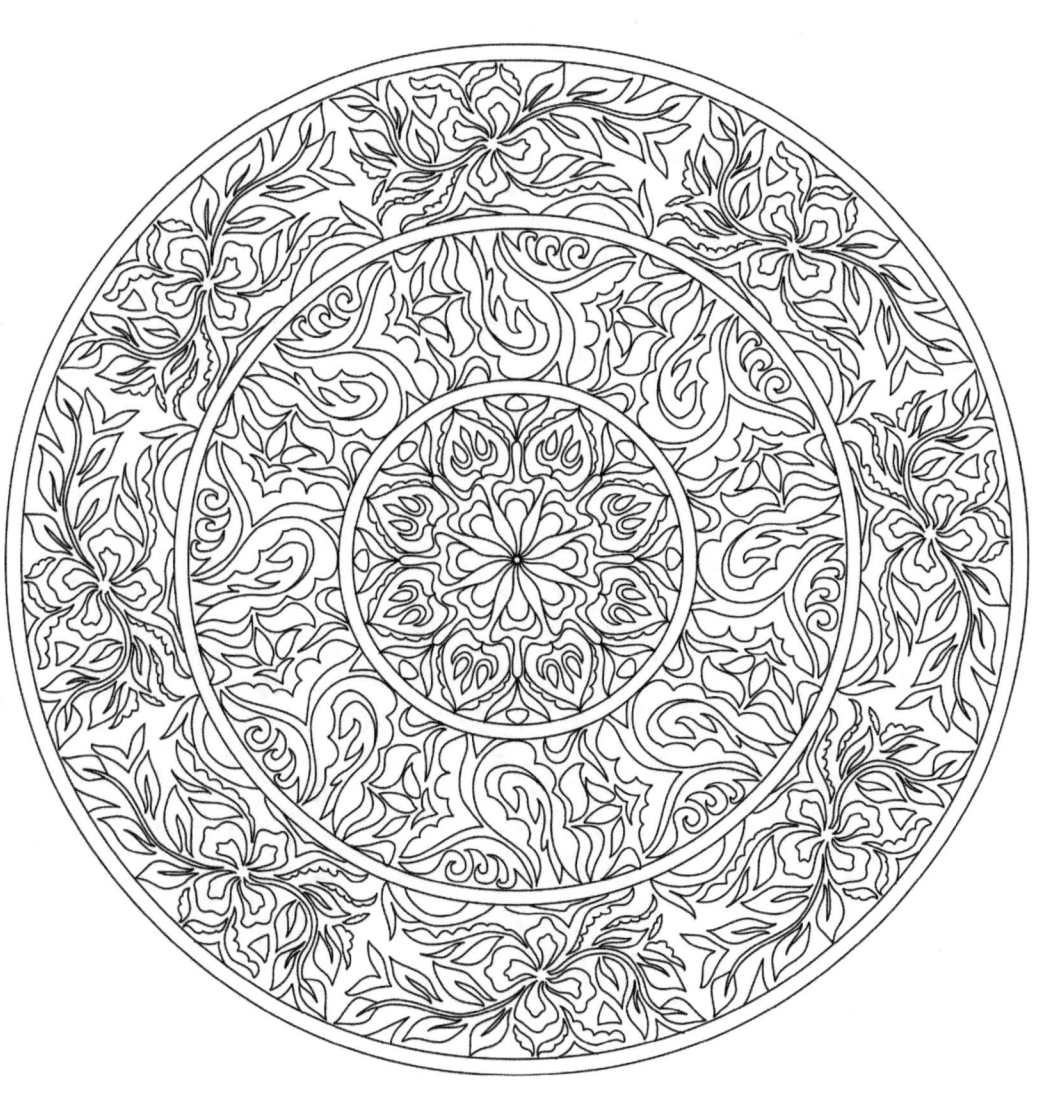

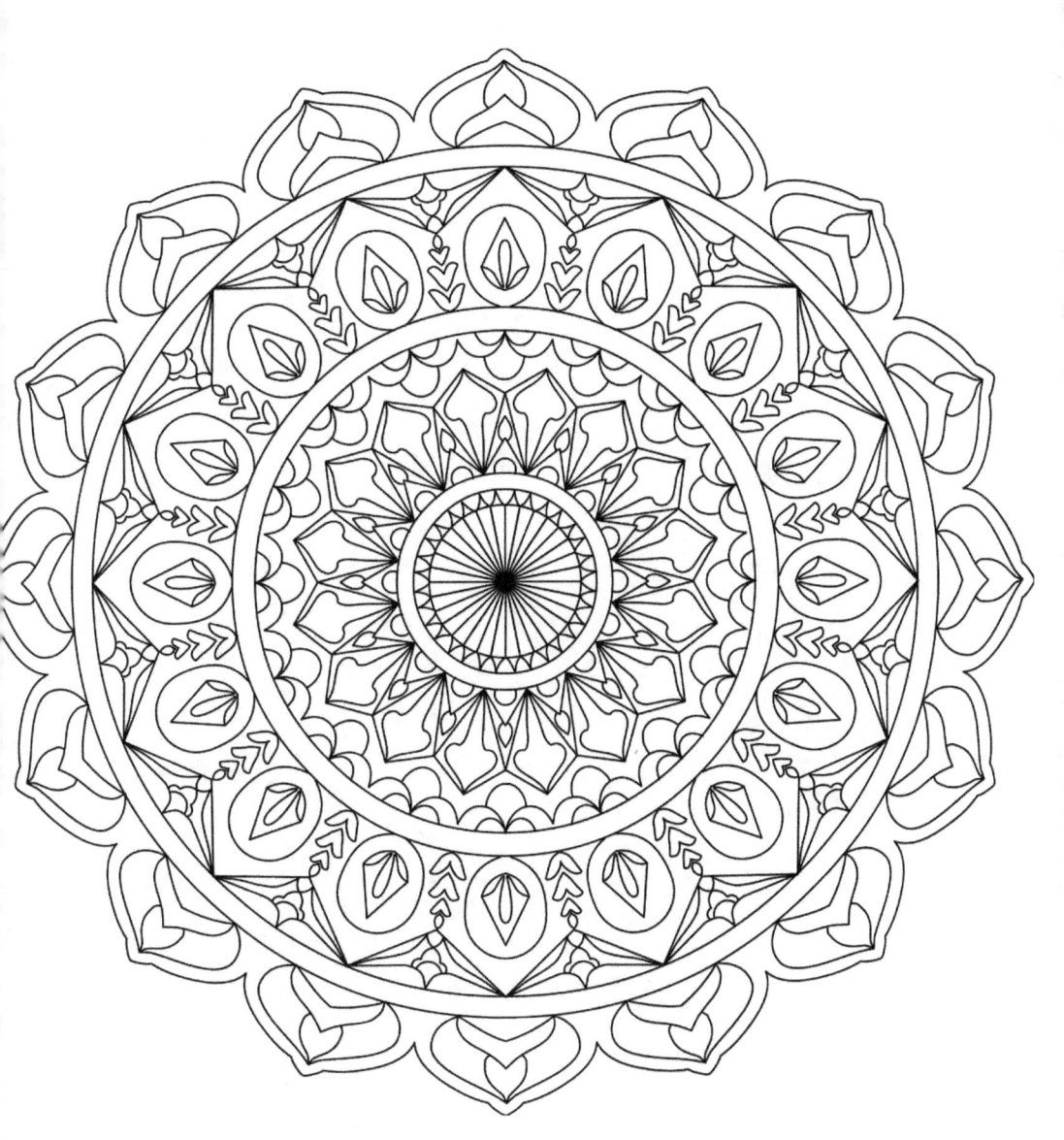

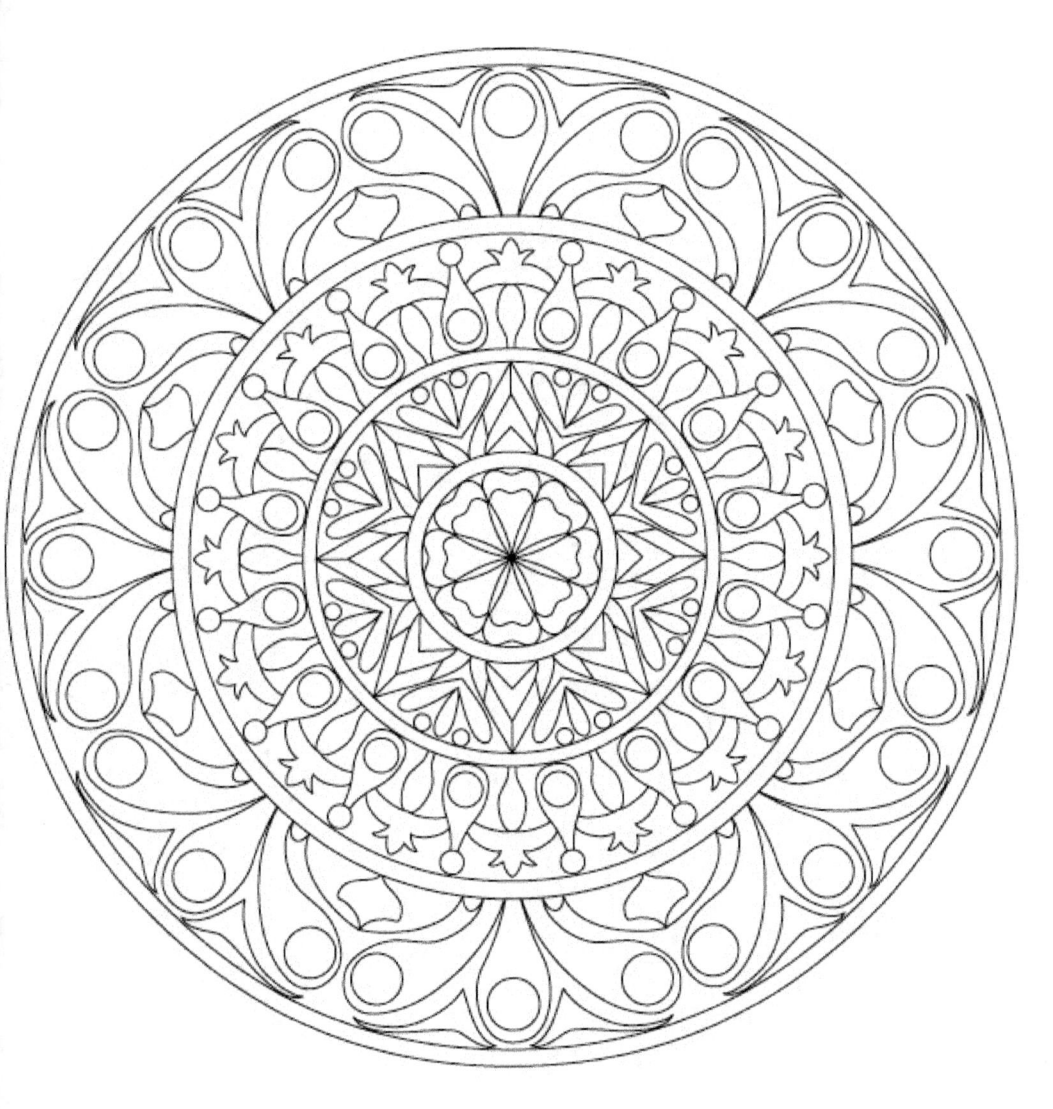

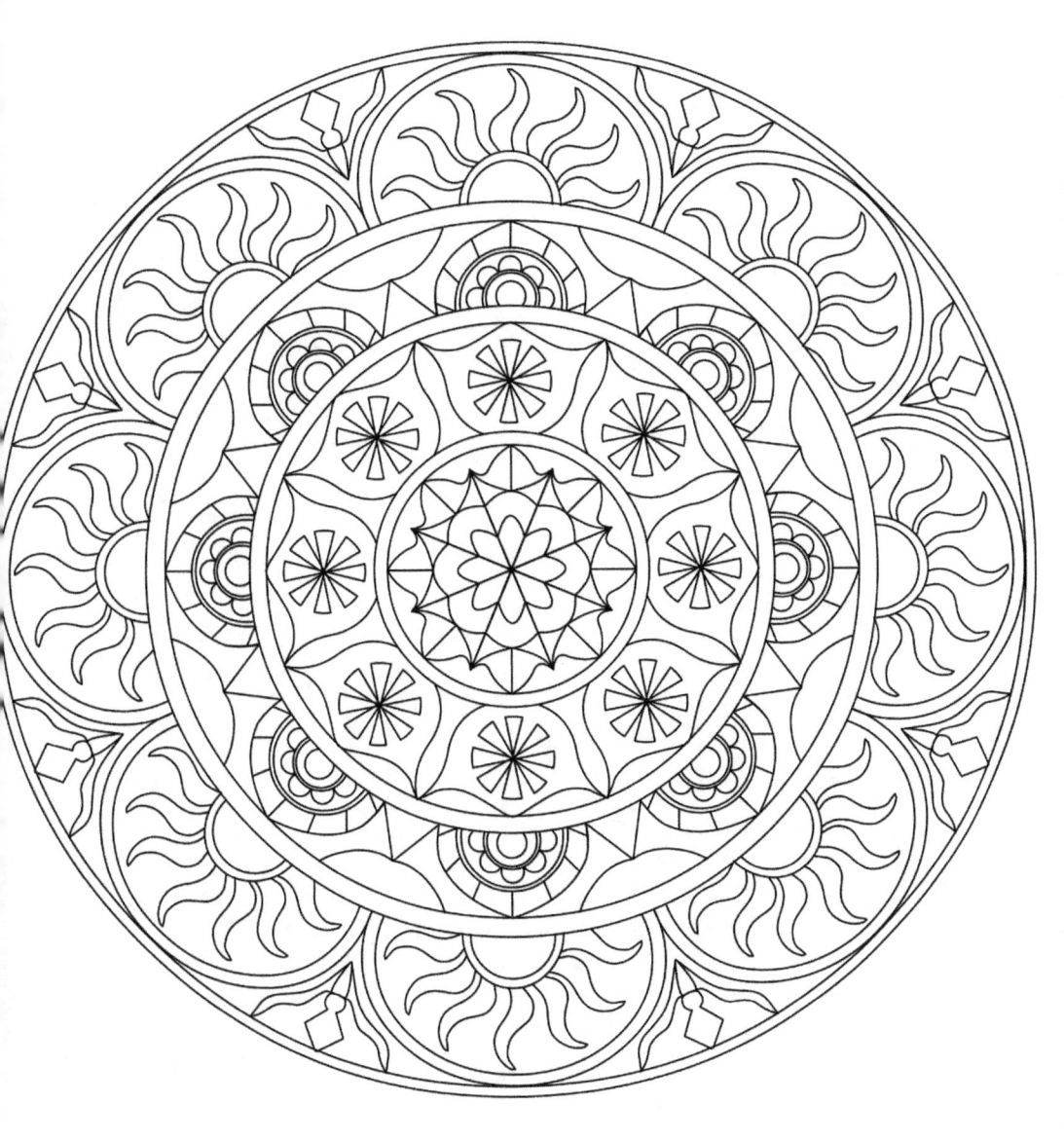

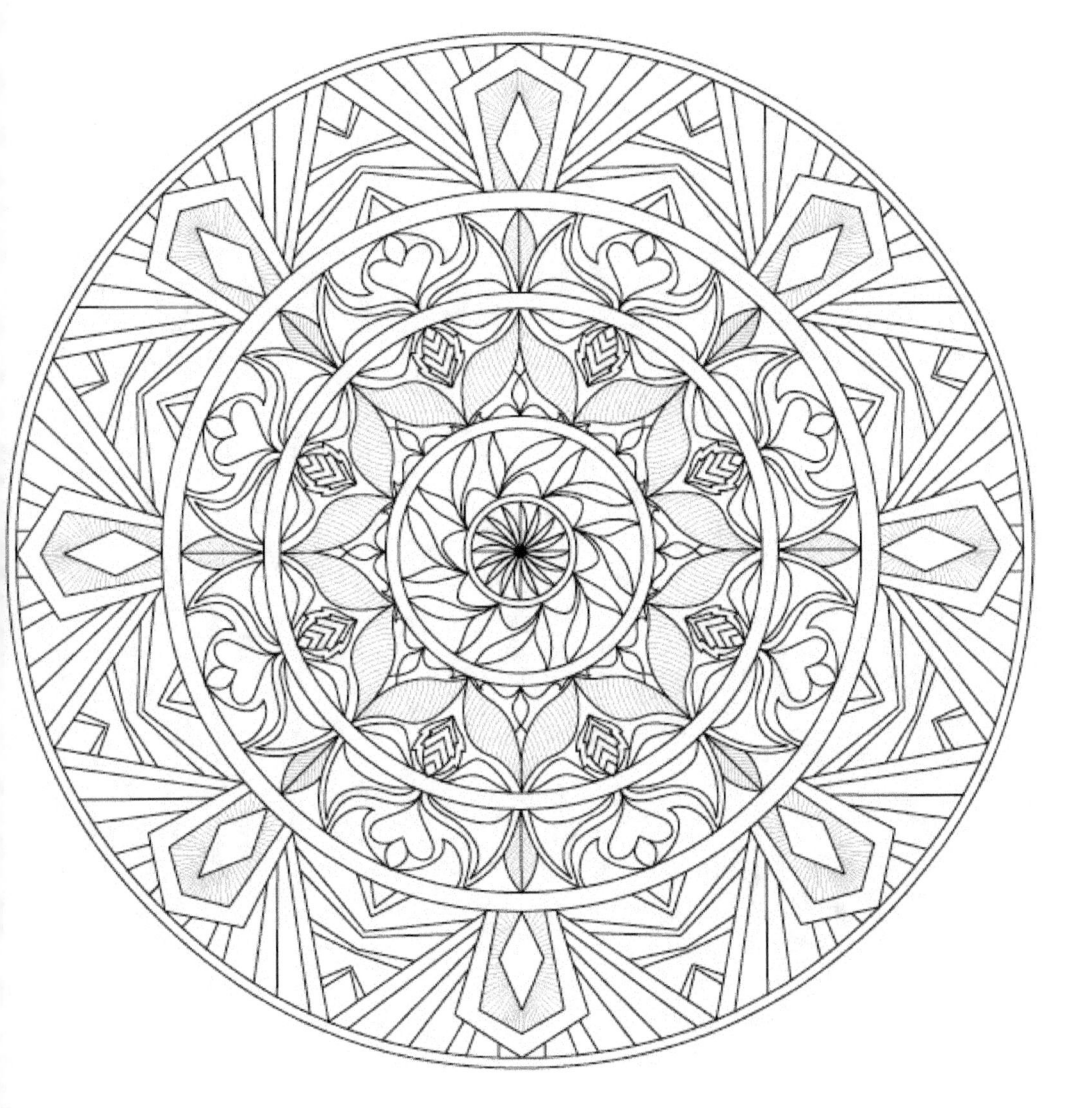

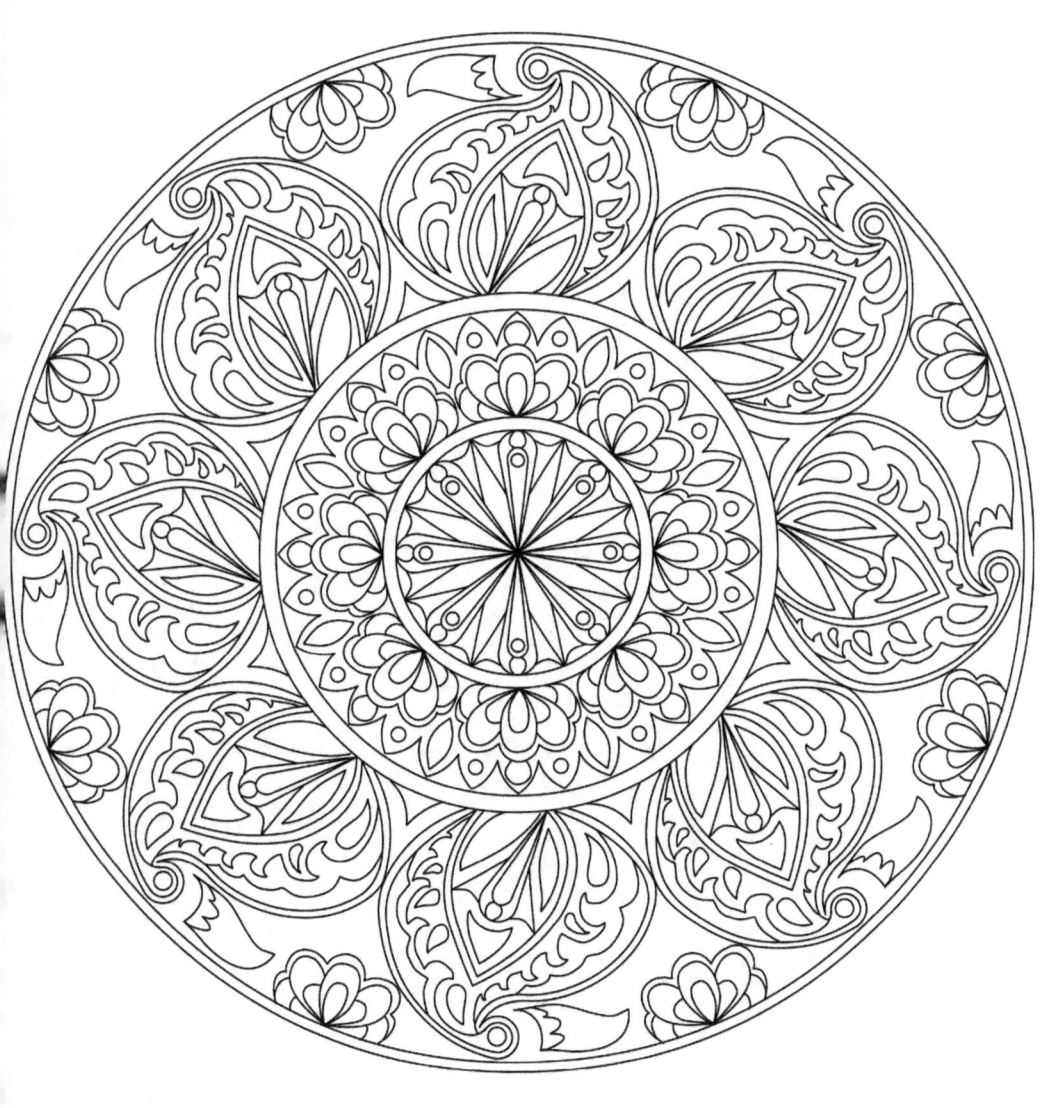

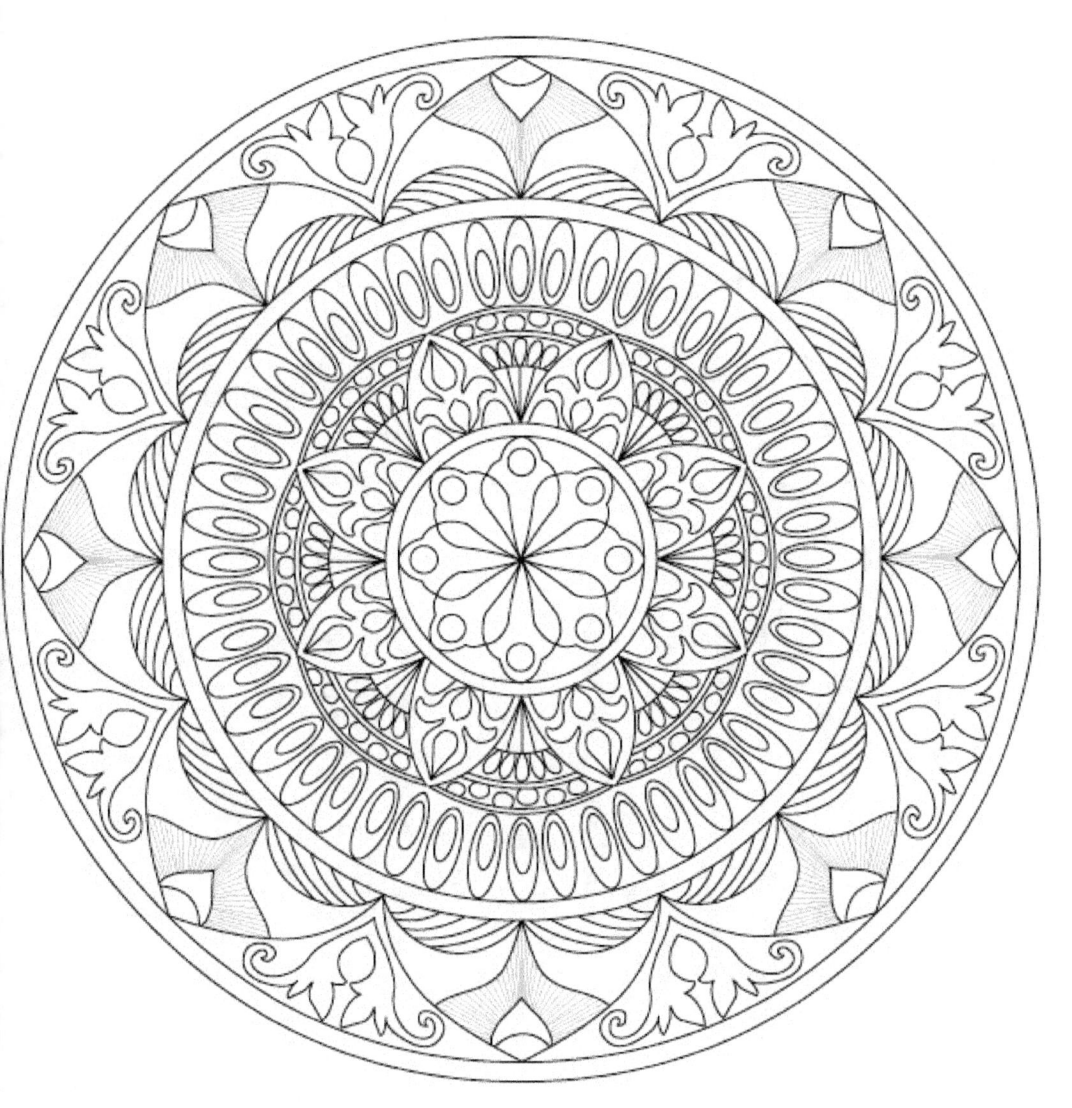

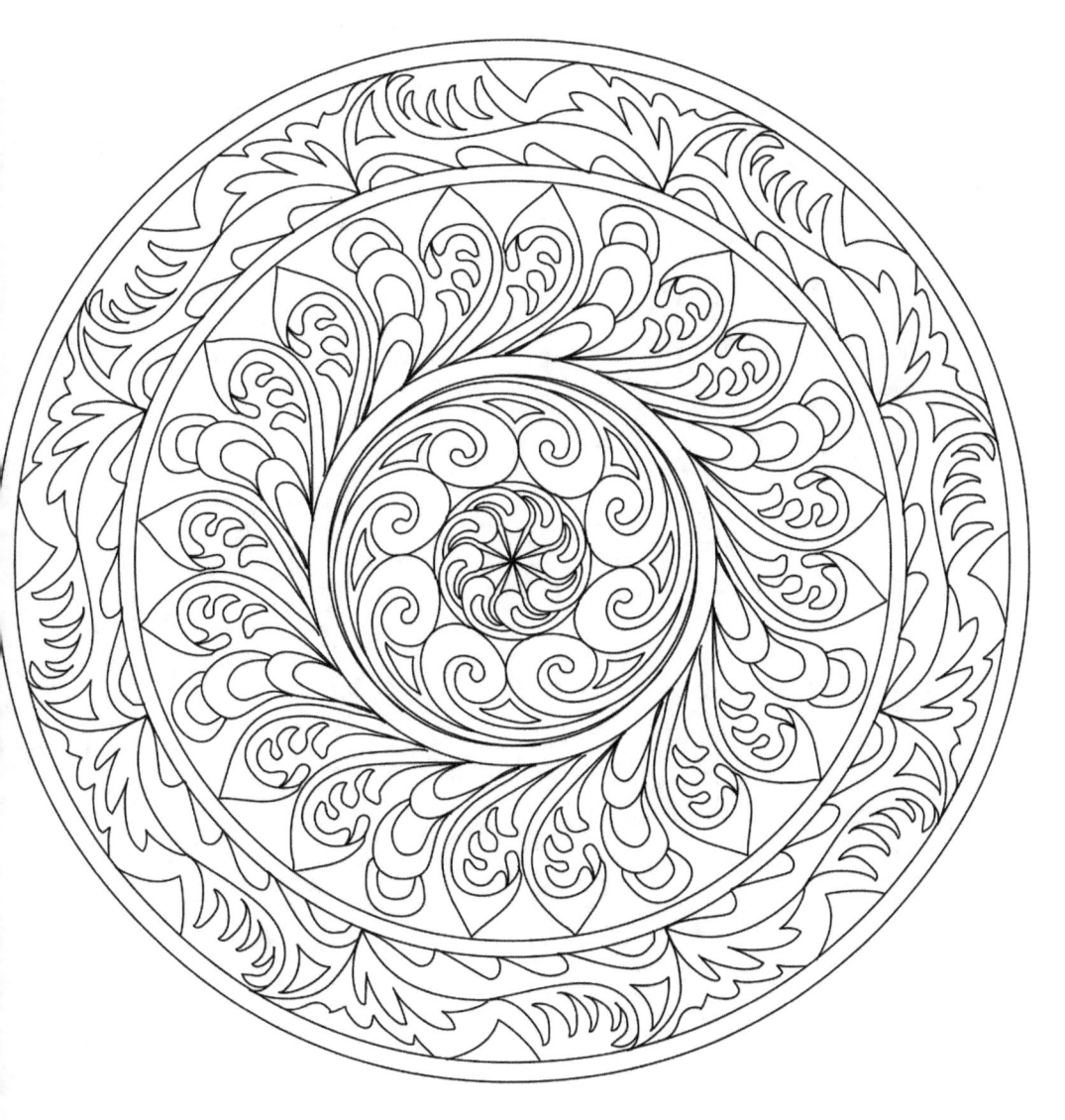

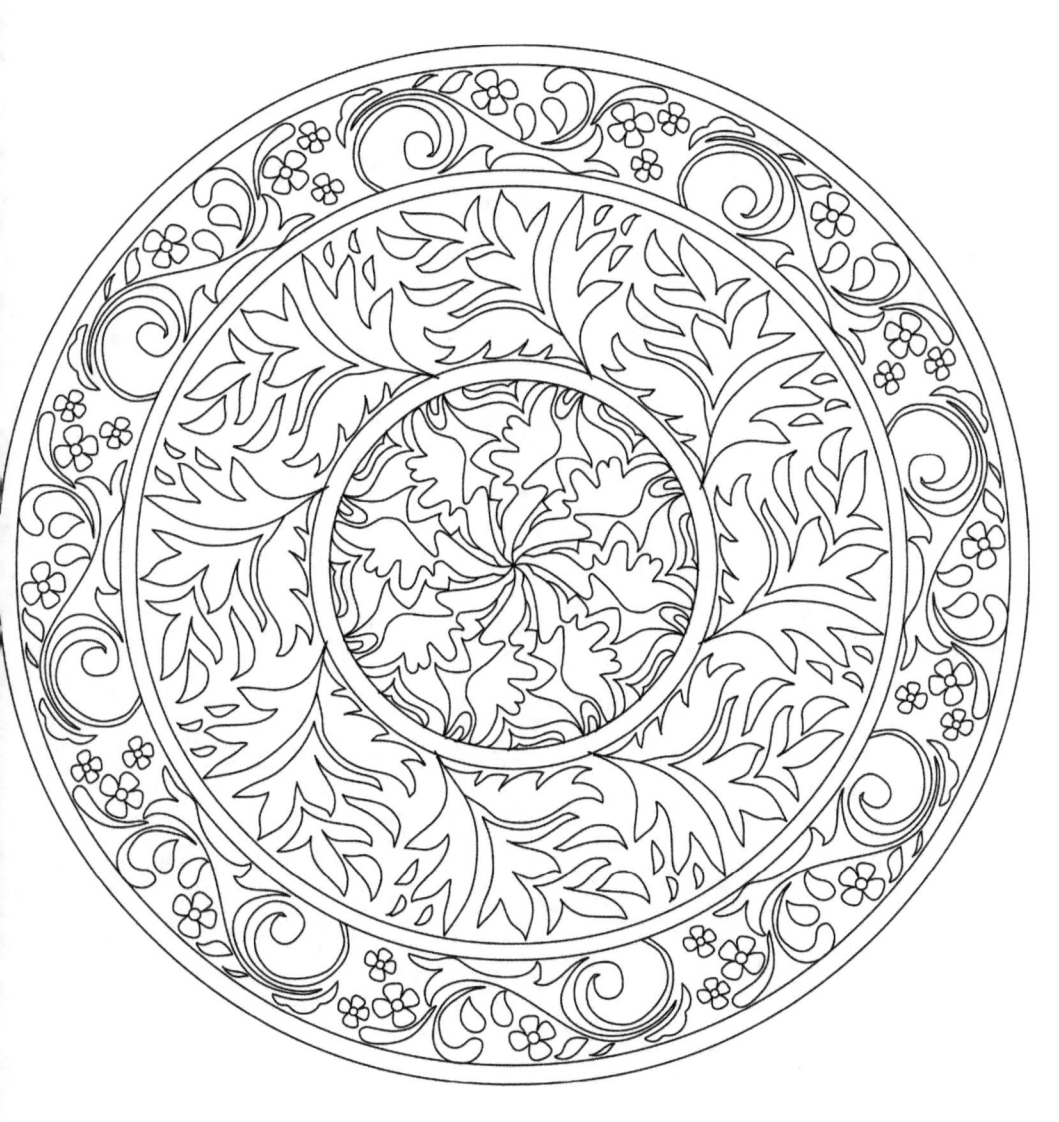

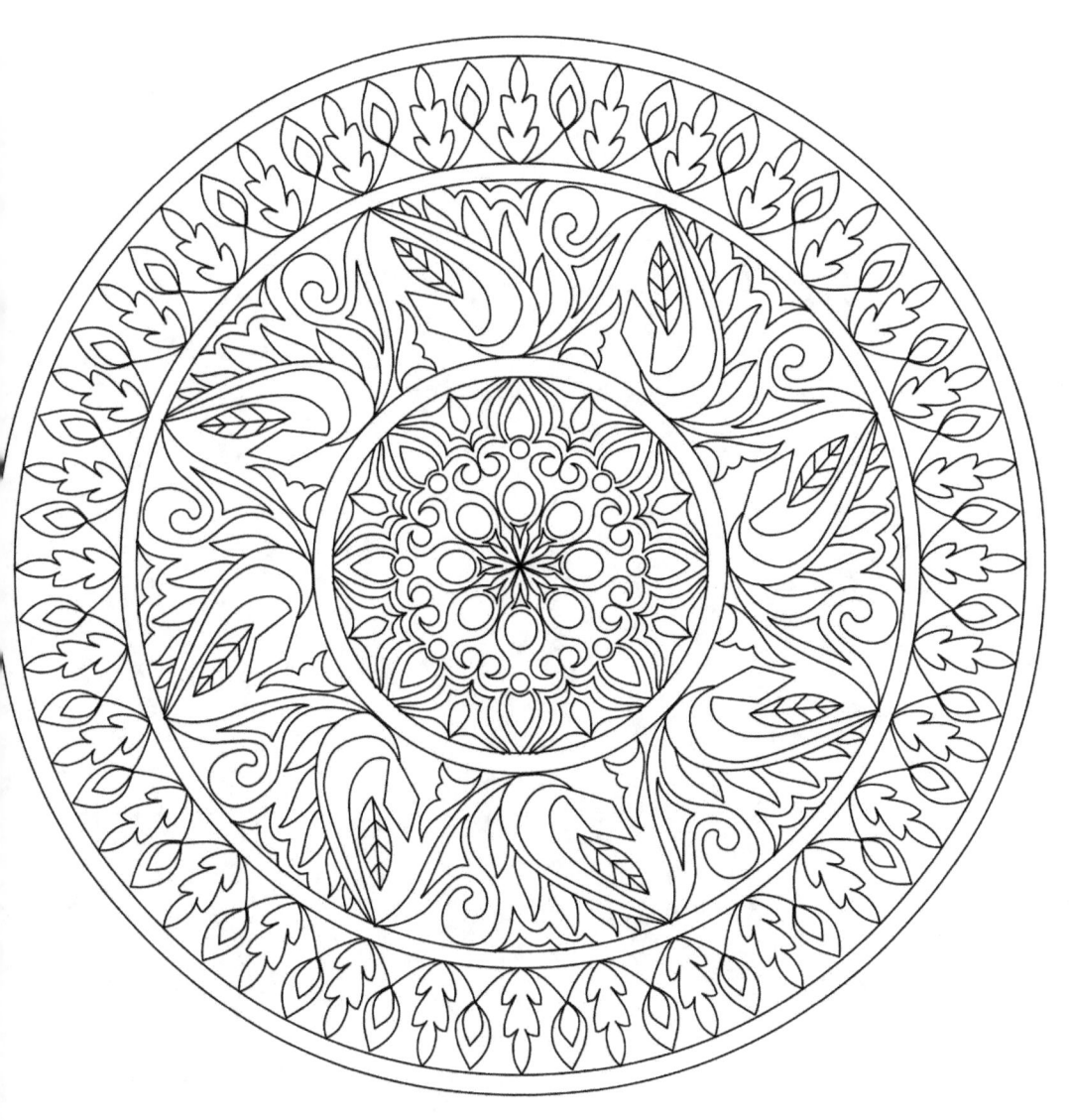

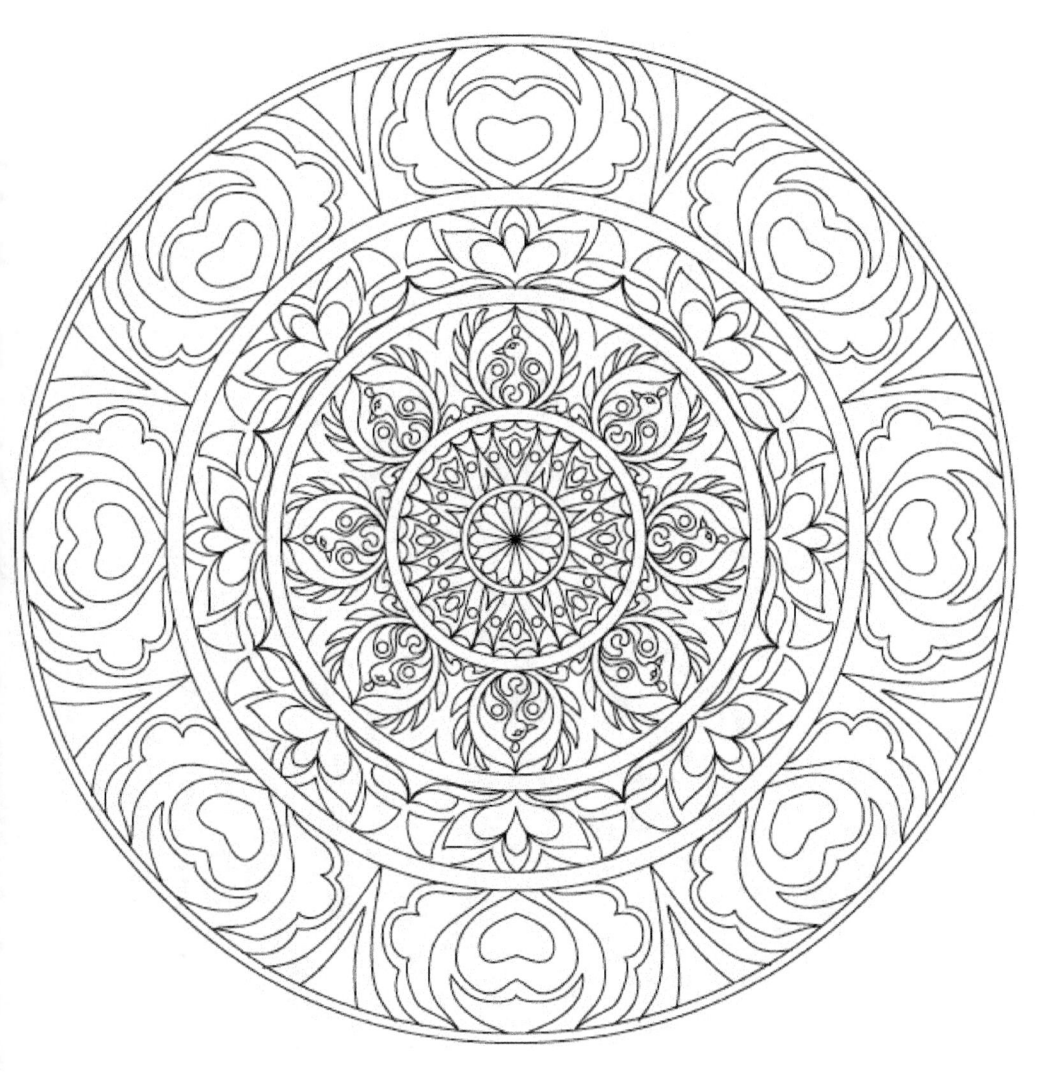

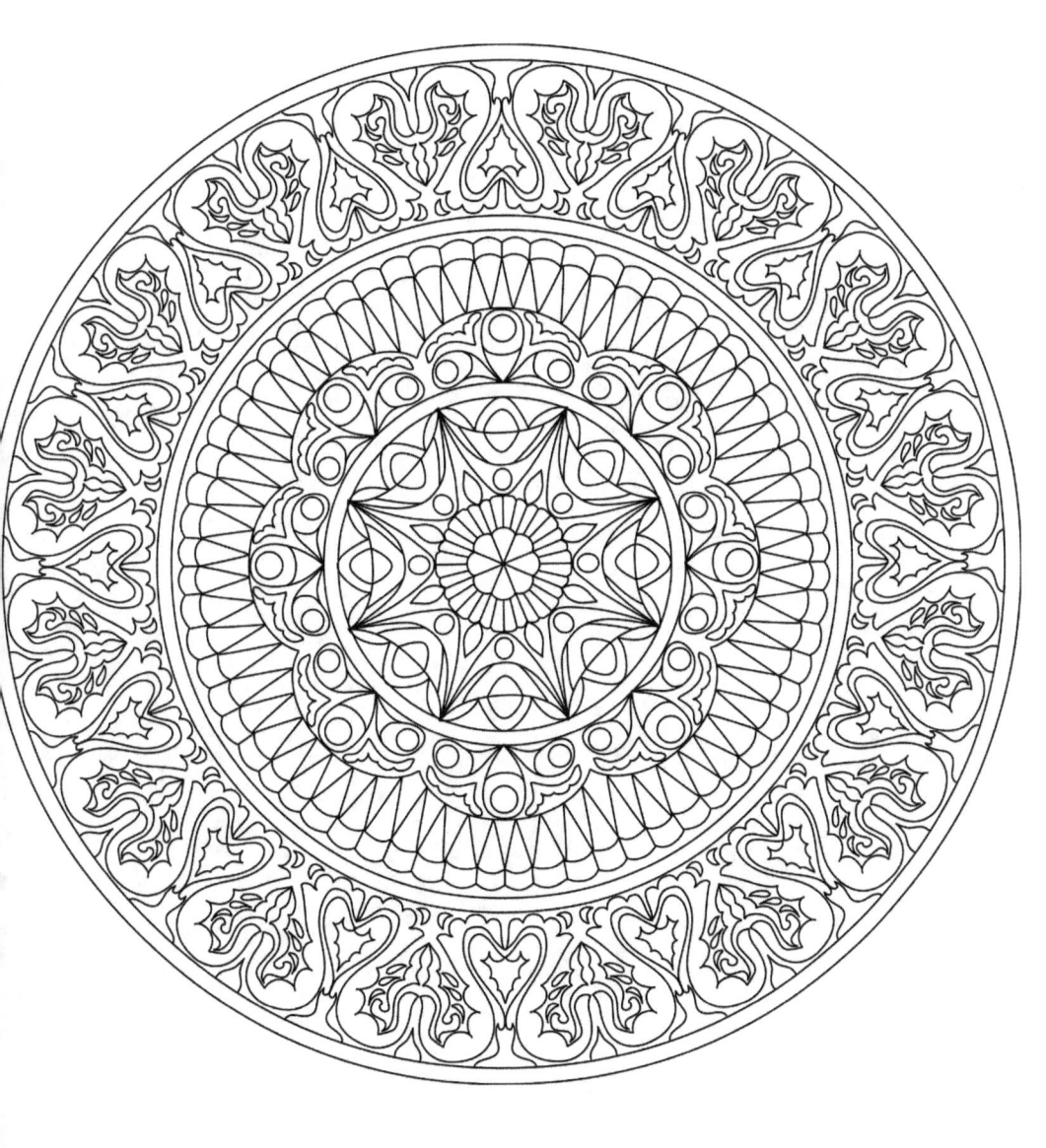

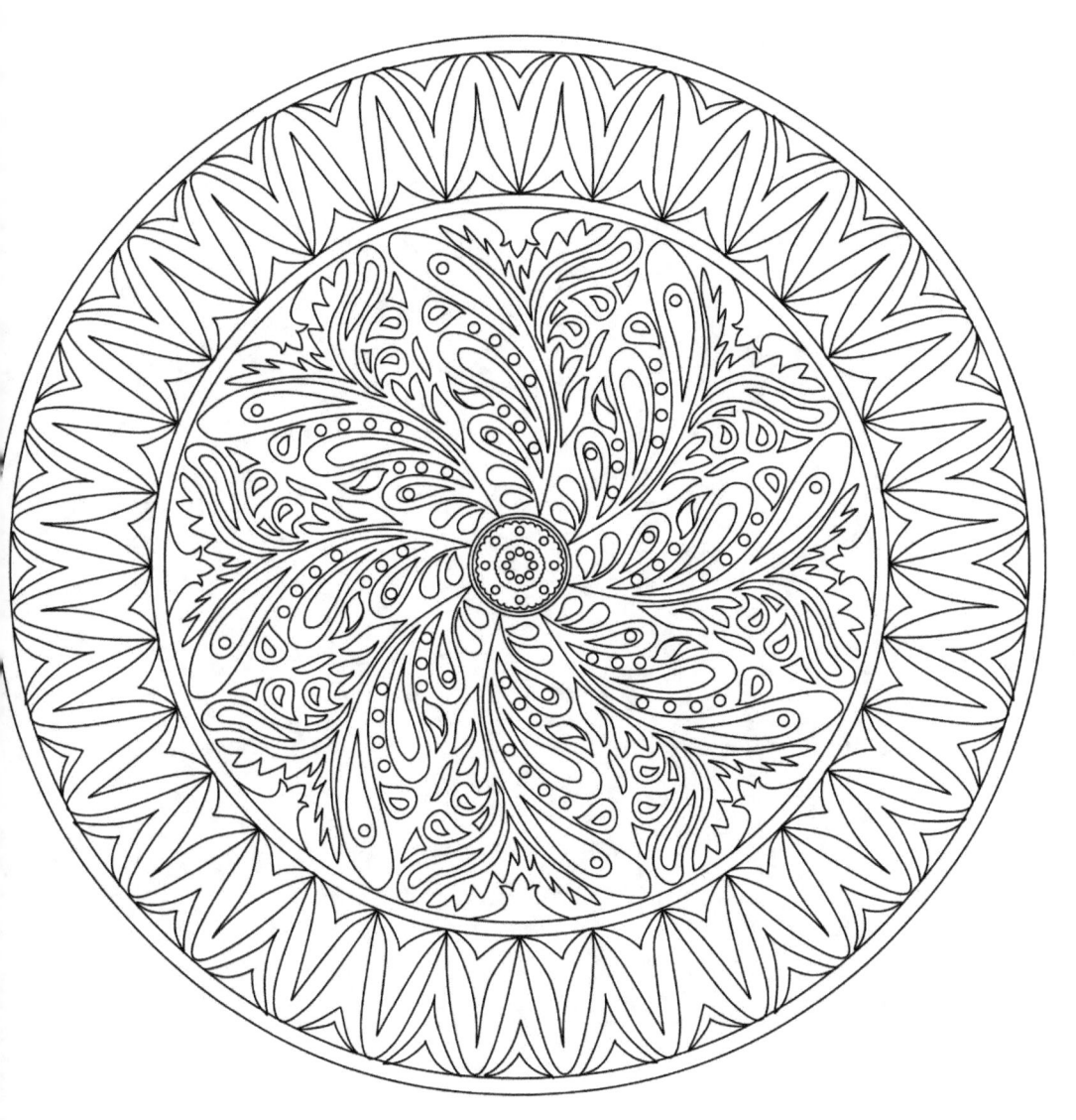

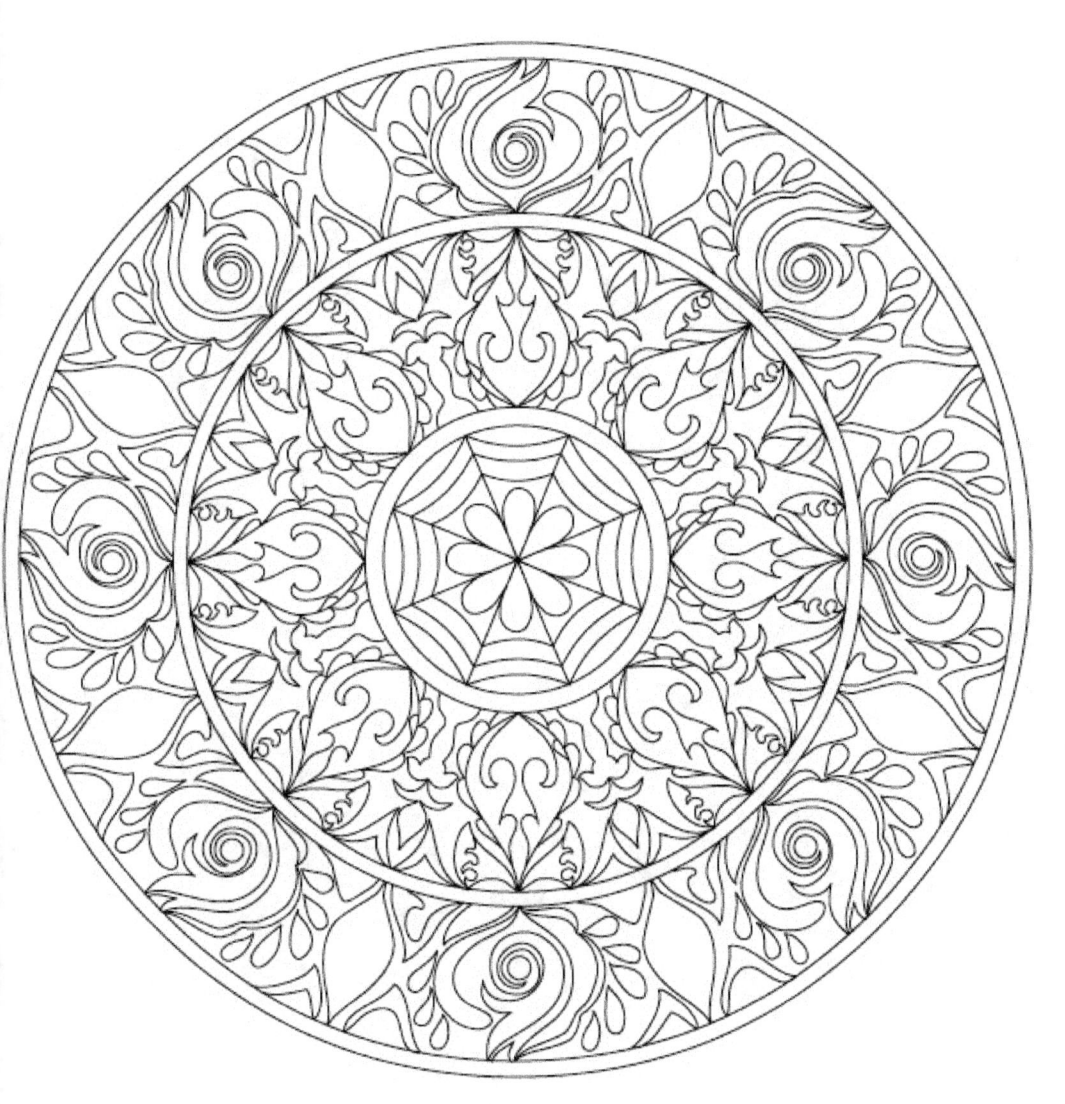

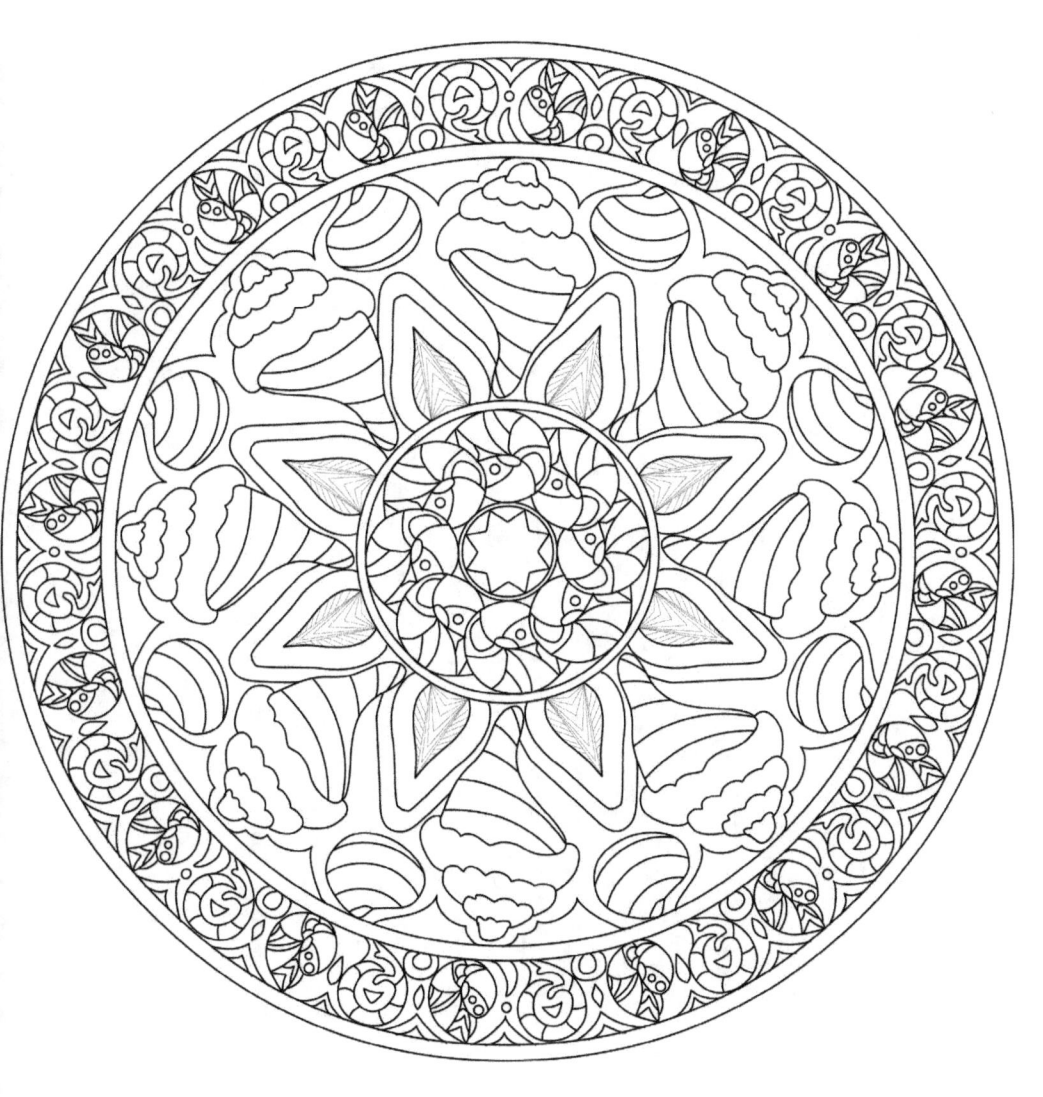

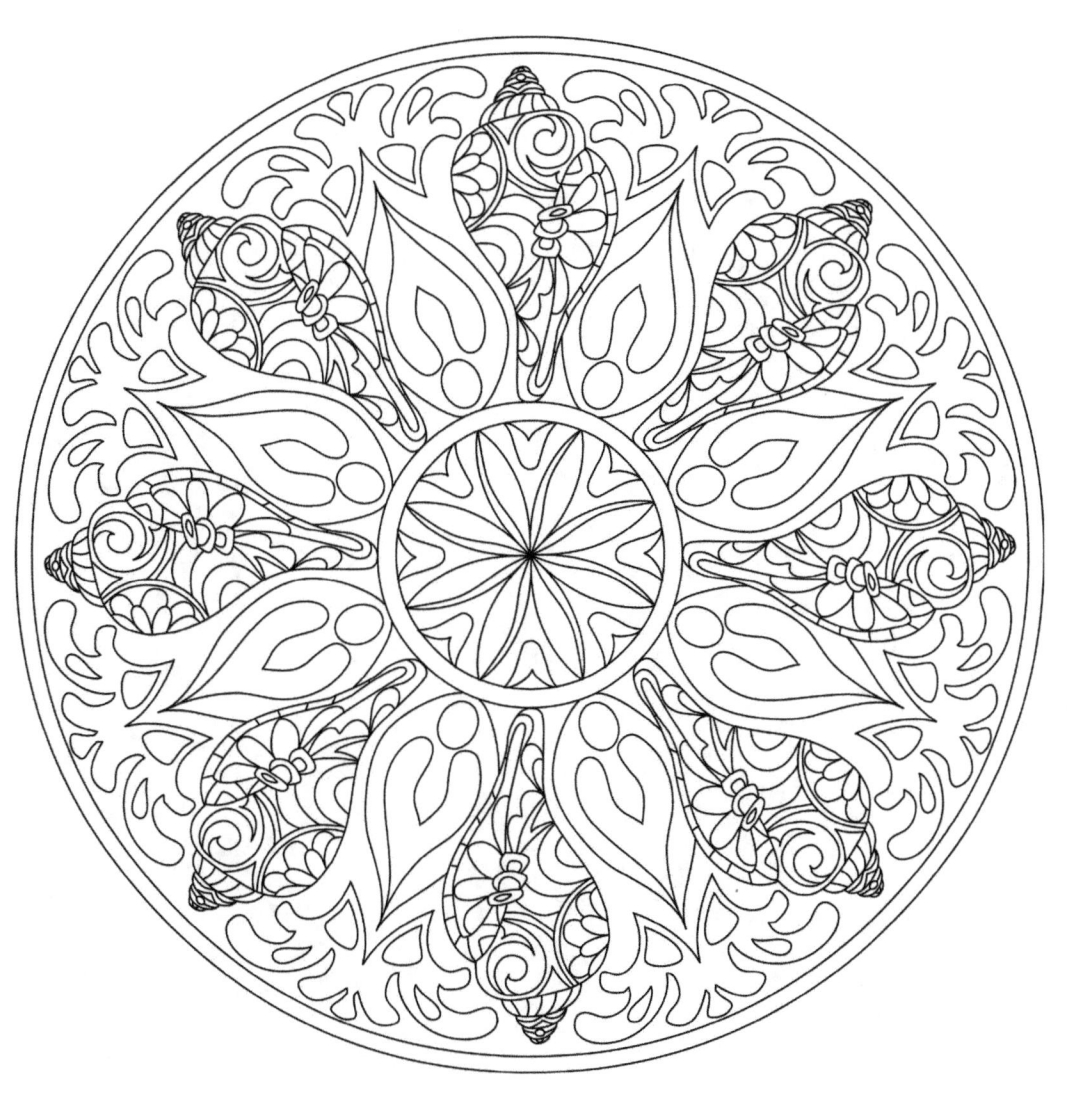

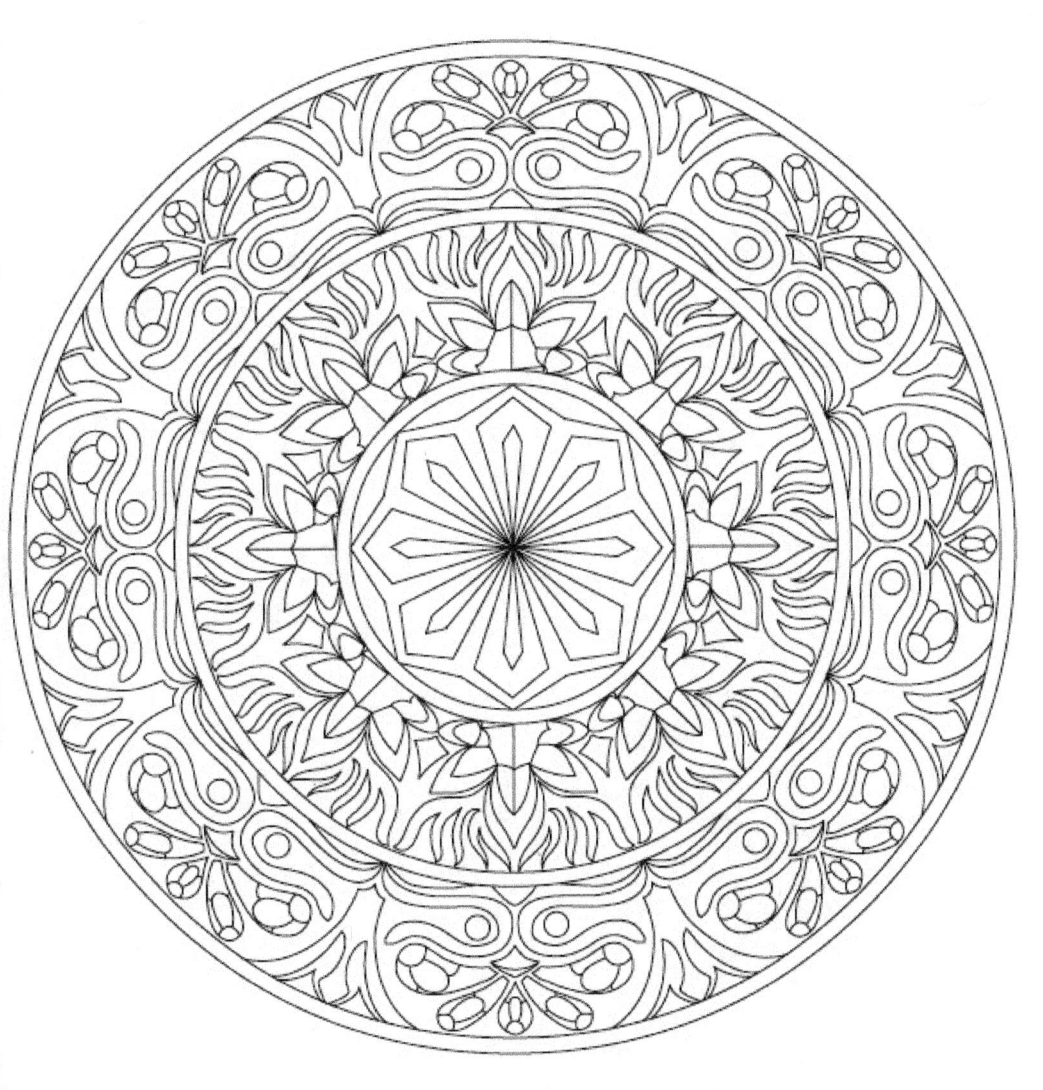

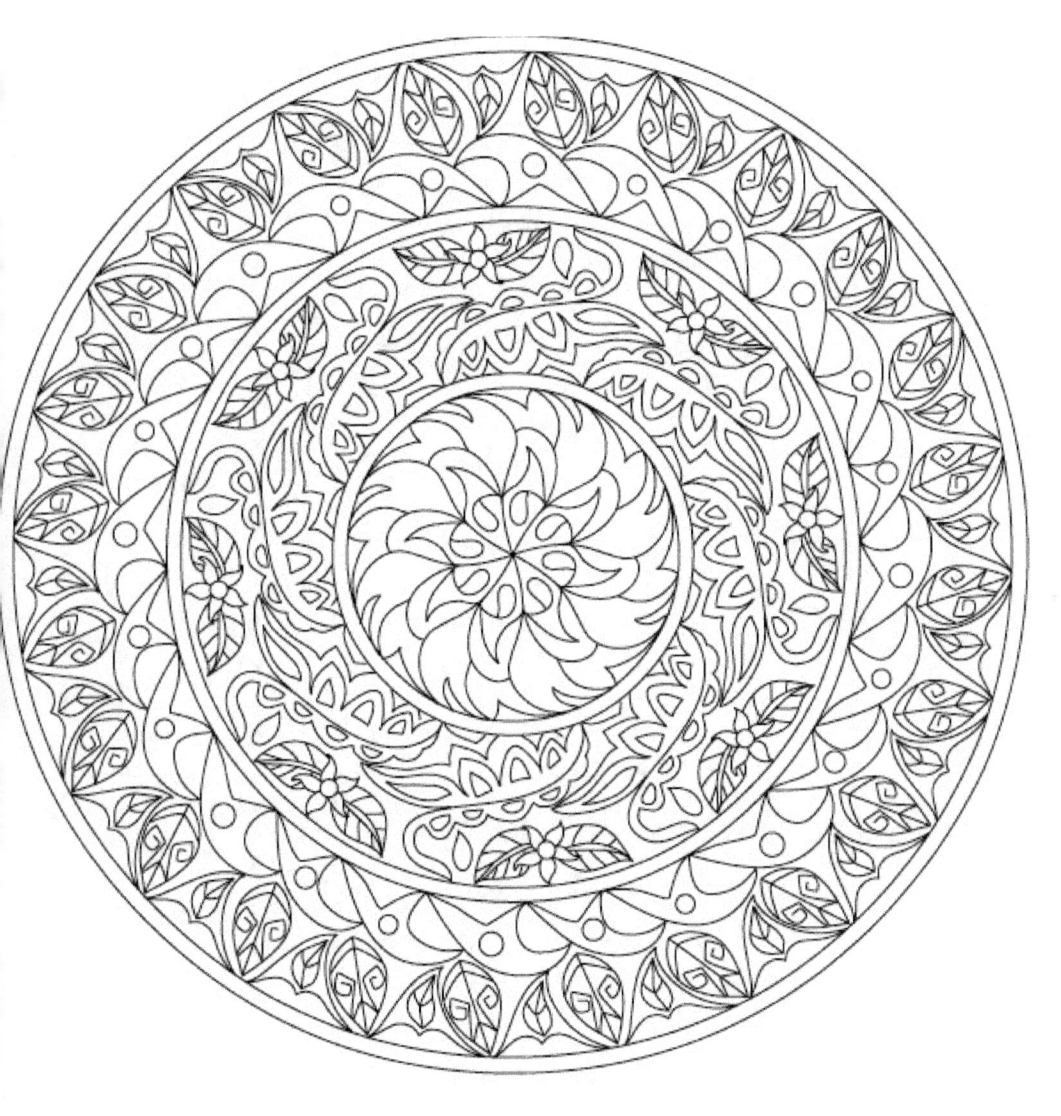

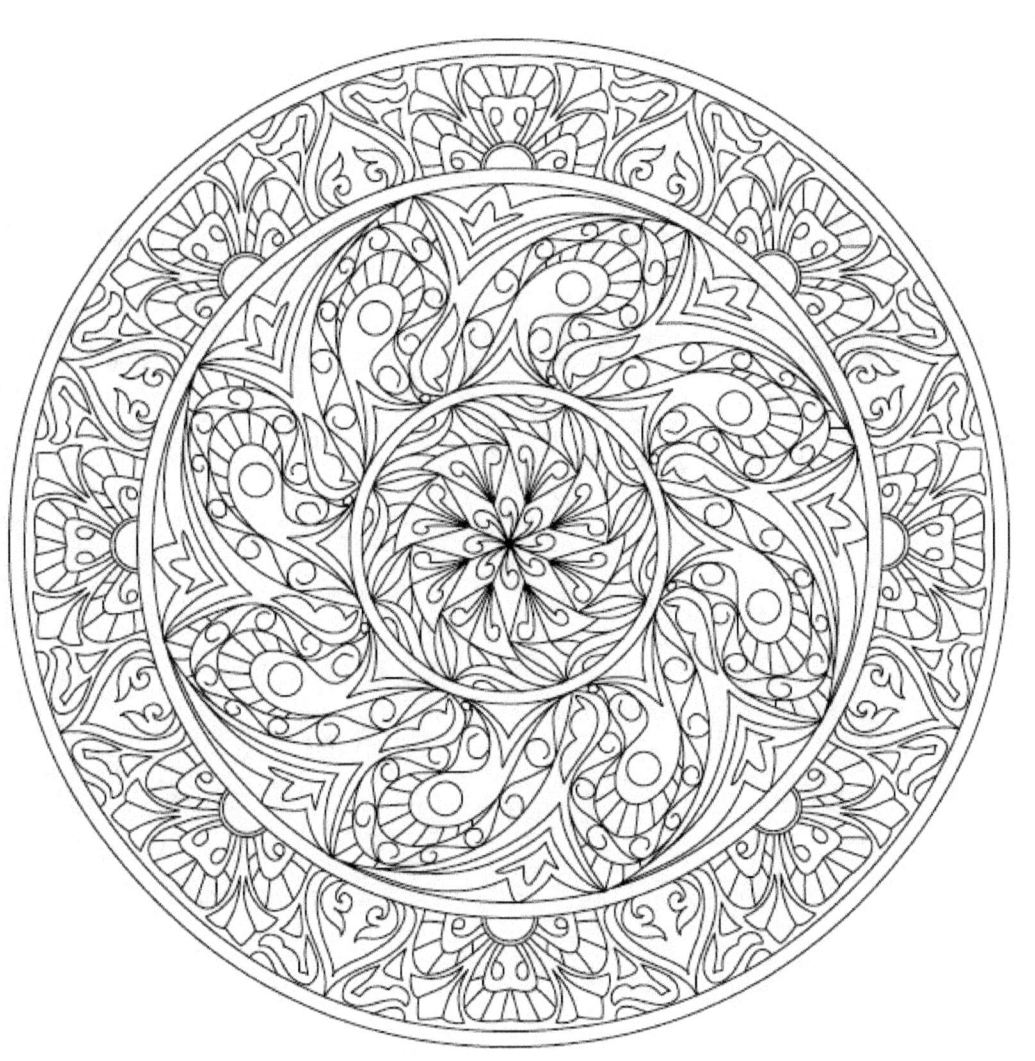

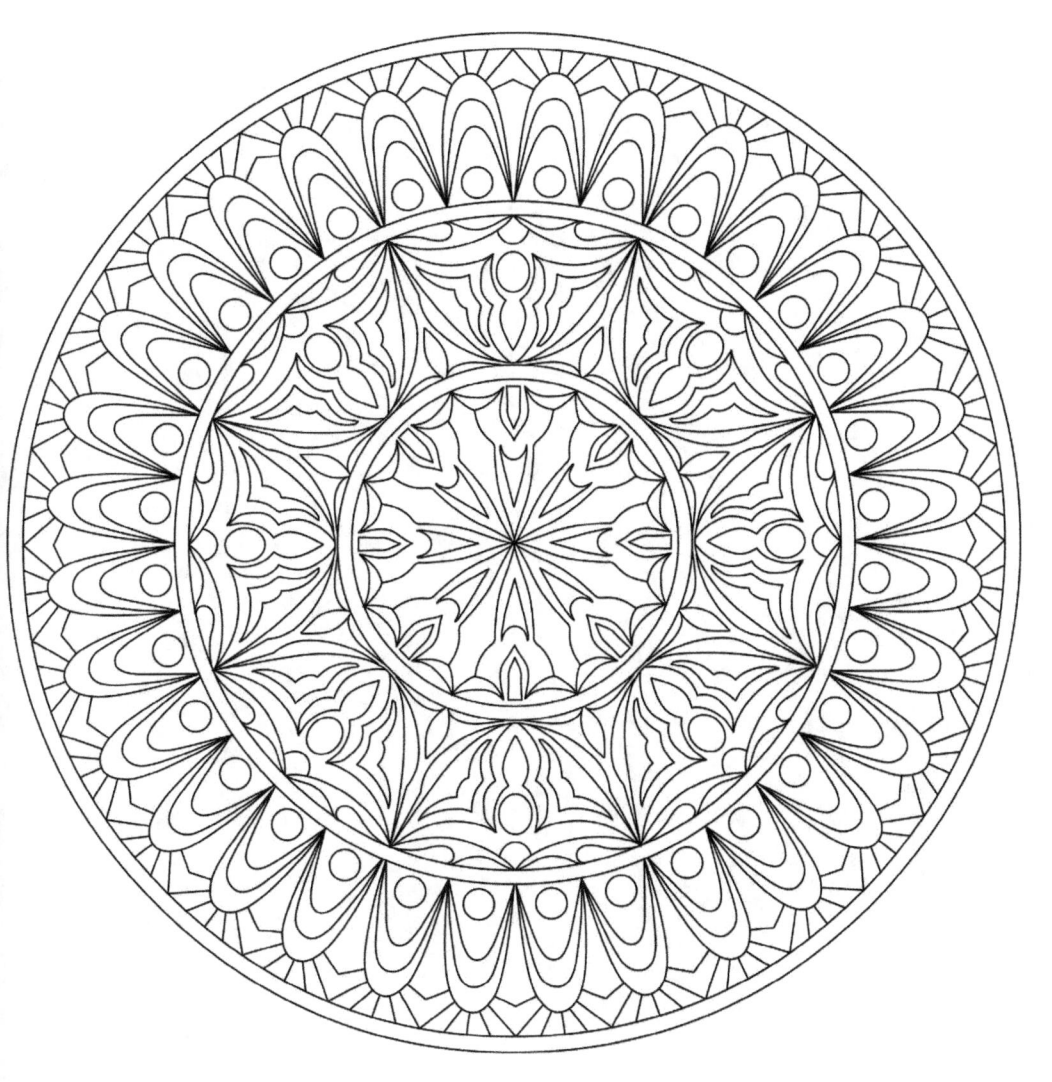

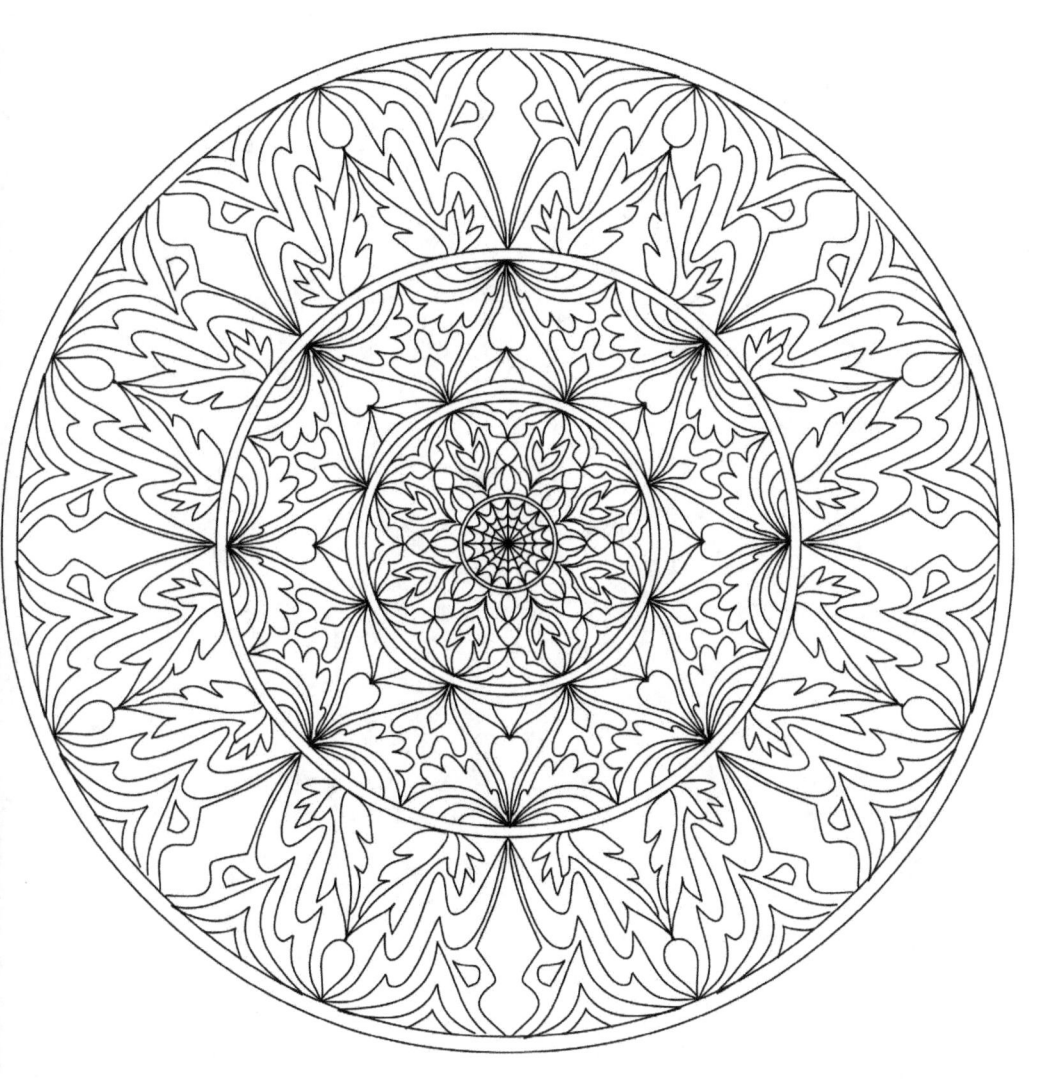

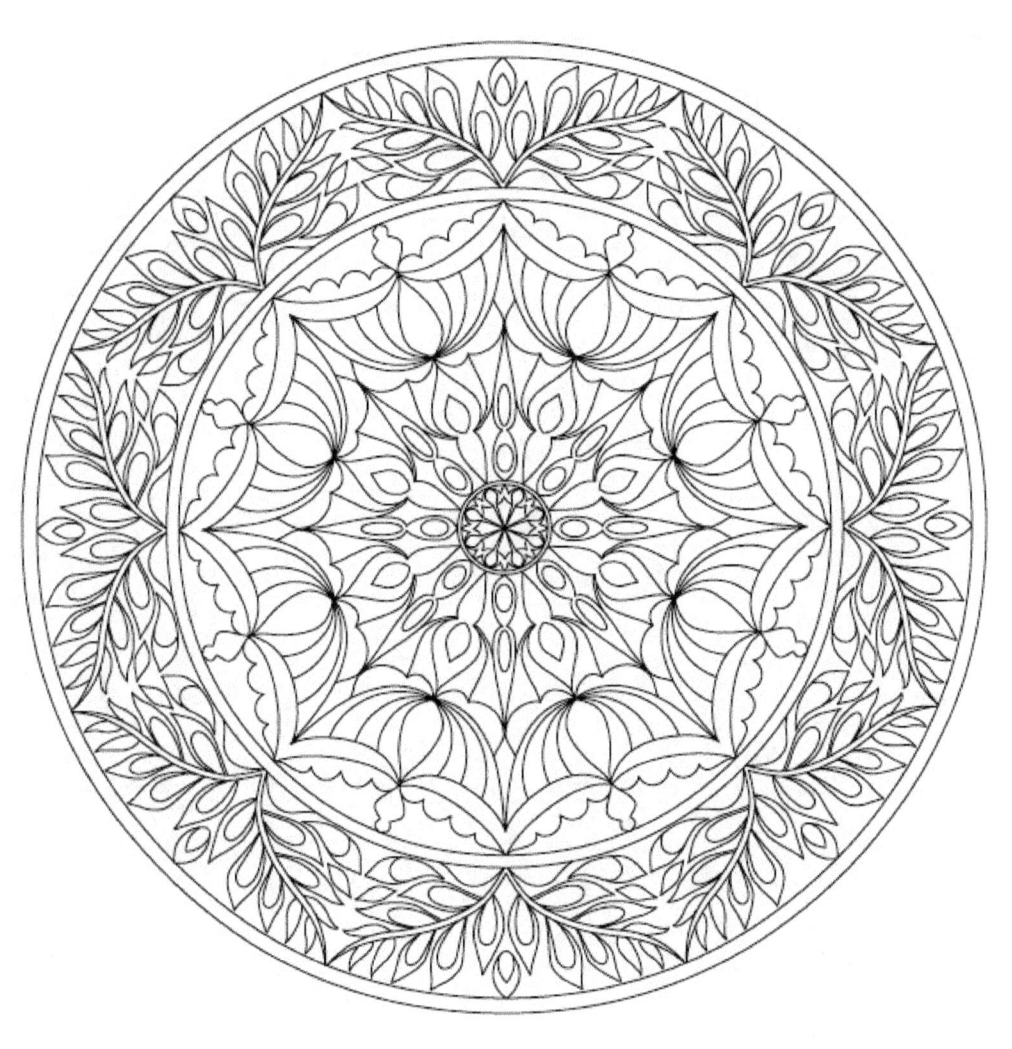

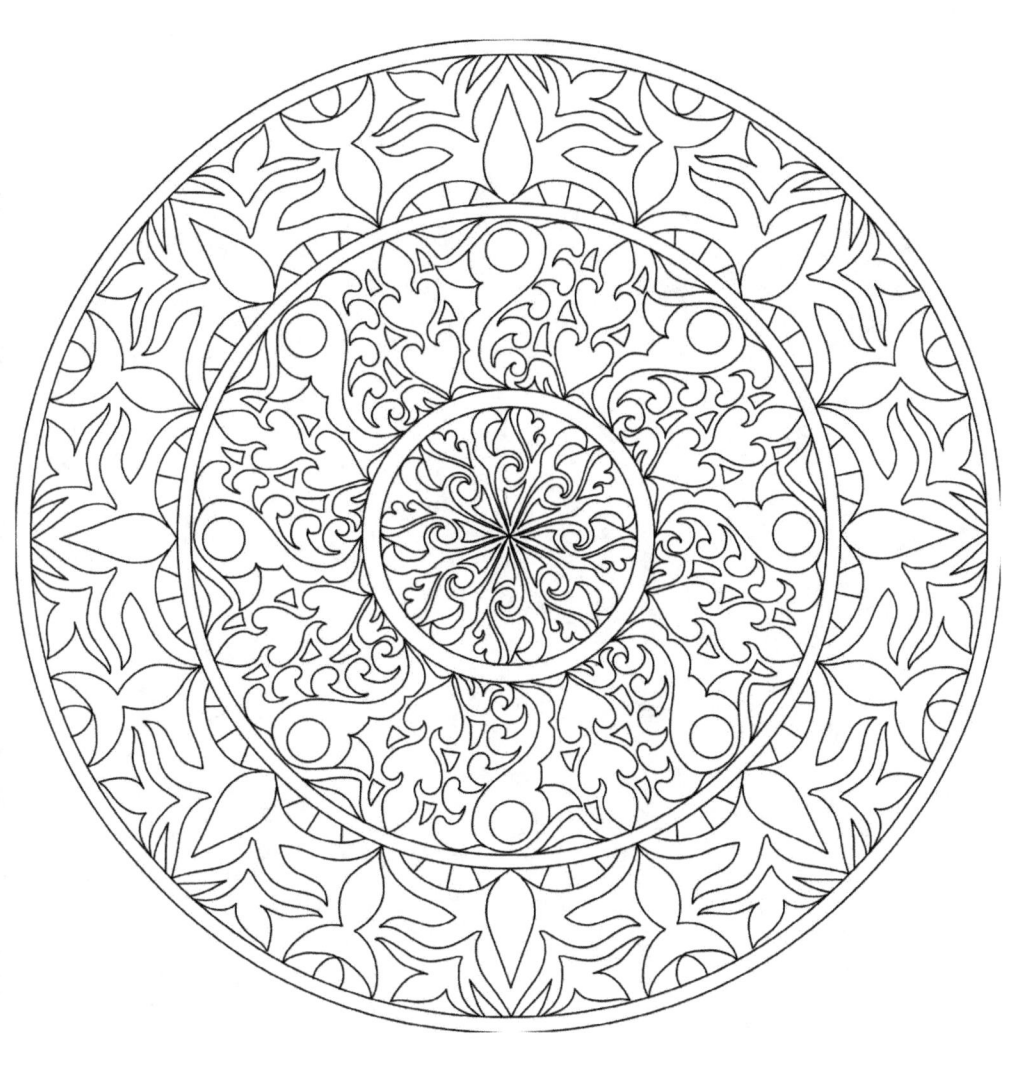

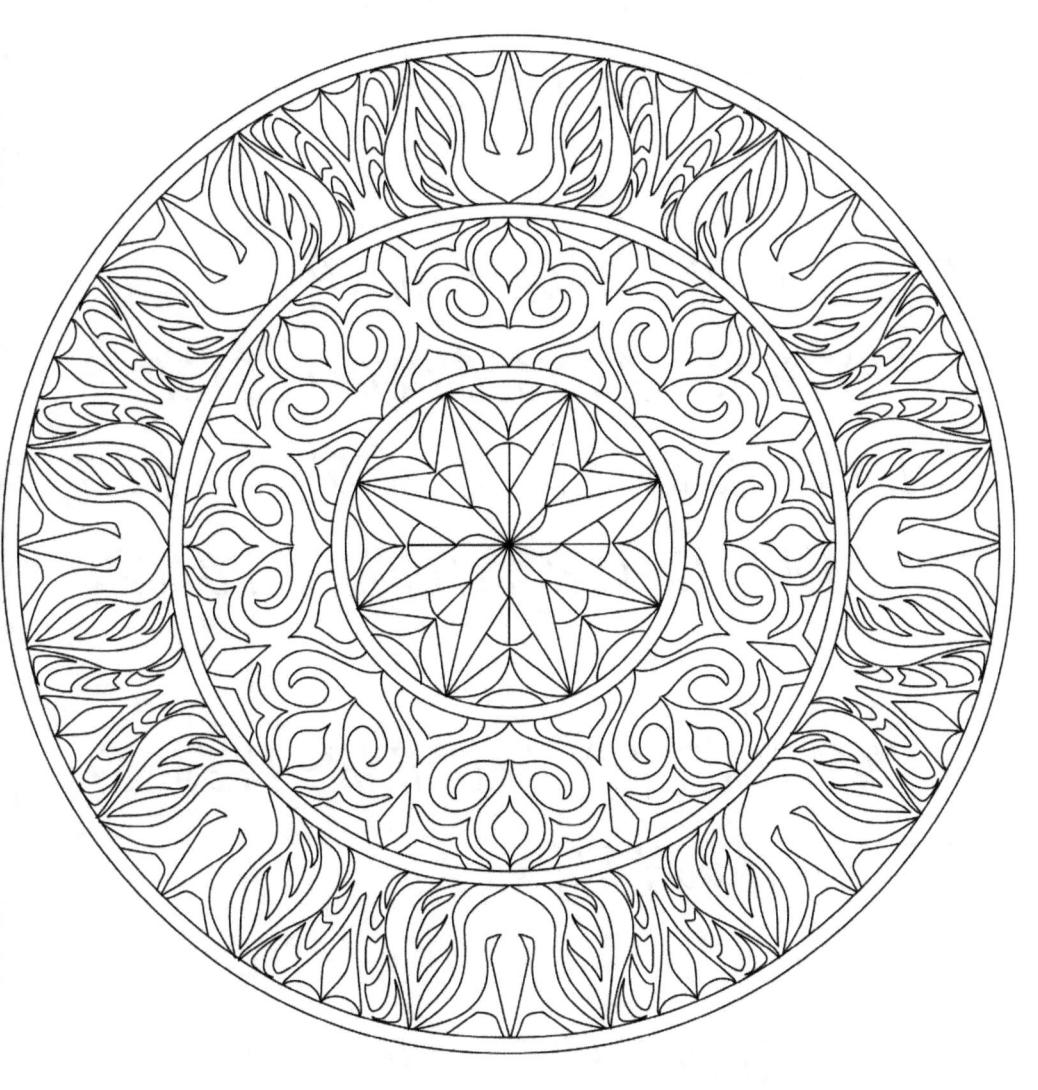

THANK YOU FOR CHOOSING A ACE COLORING TITLE

TO KEEP UP TO DATE WITH EVERYTHING ACE COLORING PLEASE FOLLOW US ON SOCIAL MEDIA OR VISIT US @ WWW.SILVERBAYPUBLISHING.COM

IF YOU HAVE ANY ENQUIRIES PLEASE GET IN TOUCH VIA:

JOE@SILVERBAYPUBLISHING.COM

www.ingramcontent.com/pod-product-compliance
Lightning Source LLC
Chambersburg PA
CBHW070947220526
45471CB00007B/2930